BRITISH
INDEPENDENT BUSES
IN THE 1990s

RICHARD STUBBINGS

AMBERLEY

First published 2019

Amberley Publishing
The Hill, Stroud
Gloucestershire, GL5 4EP

www.amberley-books.com

Copyright © Richard Stubbings, 2019

The right of Richard Stubbings to be identified
as the Author of this work has been asserted
in accordance with the Copyright, Designs and
Patents Act 1988.

ISBN 978 1 4456 8611 0 (print)
ISBN 978 1 4456 8612 7 (ebook)

British Library Cataloguing in Publication Data.
A catalogue record for this book is available from
the British Library.

Typesetting by Aura Technology and Software
Services, India. Printed in the UK.

Introduction

As the 1980s gave way to the 1990s, we started to see the results of deregulation take root. The former NBC companies, which were now privately owned, began to be swallowed up into larger groupings such as Stagecoach and the forerunners of Arriva, Go-Ahead and First. These groups also began to take over the former municipal companies, as well as absorbing a number of well-known independent operators.

This volume, illustrated with photographs from the collection I have built up over the years, shows the changing face of independent operators during this period. We see companies competing fiercely with each other in the larger conurbations such as Sheffield and Manchester. We also see operators working to expand their existing operations and growing in size as a result of that – Tillingbourne Services in the Guildford area is a good example of this. London was becoming a more colourful place as private operators gained franchises to operate specific routes. Other companies carried on working in much the same way as they had always done, especially perhaps in the more rural areas. Inevitably some firms fell by the wayside, some through takeover, as with a few well-known names such as South Notts, taken over by Nottingham City Transport in 1991, Stevensons passing to British Bus in 1994, later to become Arriva, and OK Motor Services passing to the Go-Ahead group in 1995. In East Anglia, well-known firms like Norfolks of Nayland and Partridge of Hadleigh joined with Hedingham & District. Others ceased trading for a variety of reasons, such as Blue Saloon in Guildford, taken over by London & Country, and Hants & Sussex in Emsworth, who were eventually absorbed by Southampton Citybus. Others carried on with minimal outward change, such as Safeguard in Guildford. It had been feared that many country services would disappear as a result of deregulation. The traditional market day services, operated by many a small rural company, had by now largely disappeared, mainly through people's changing lifestyles and the use of the car. However, studies showed that rural bus services had been more or less maintained at their pre-deregulation levels.

Away from bus operation, independent operators of all sizes were still very active in coaching work, with private hires, tours and participating in express operations, often in conjunction with National Express. Coaches were also now being built to a higher specification, with reduced seating for extra comfort, video players and other luxuries.

The vehicles being operated were beginning to change. The major success story of the 1990s has to have been the Dennis Dart. In its first incarnation, nearly 3,500 Darts were sold to companies both big and small. During the 1990s, however, there was an increasing move towards vehicles that were more accessible to those who had impaired mobility, resulting in low-floor vehicles entering service. The first generation Dart was replaced by the Dart SLF. By the end of its production run, over 9,000 Dart SLFs had been built in a variety of lengths. During the 1990s an ever increasing number of these vehicles were entering service with independent operators, a number of which are illustrated within these pages. Other manufacturers were also gaining a foothold, such as Optare. However, there was a still a large number of second-hand vehicles – sometimes fairly youthful, others less so – continuing service with independent operators. Some second-hand vehicles became very popular with some operators, such as the Bristol RE, in turn making these companies very popular with enthusiasts. Certainly, the RE brings back many memories of journeys to and from school for me. There are also a number of examples in these pages of the lives of vehicles being increased through rebuilding and rebodying, including double-deckers rebodied as single-deckers and coaches similarly treated.

By the 1990s I was firmly based in the south-east of England, but still making frequent trips back to my roots in the West Country to visit family, my parents having now retired to Cornwall. This may, perhaps, help to explain the large number of photographs from these areas. Some places, such as Wales and Scotland, unfortunately do not feature, purely as a result of lack of opportunity. However, other opportunities to visit places with which I was less familiar did present themselves, such as the North West and the North East.

Once again, I must acknowledge the information gleaned online from Bus Data and from Wikipedia as extremely useful sources of detailed information on a number of aspects. In addition, the information gleaned from my collection of *Buses Annuals*, *Buses Yearbooks* and *Buses* magazines has been invaluable at filling in gaps in my knowledge. I hope very much that you enjoy my wanderings around the country, camera in hand!

The smart red and cream vehicles of Safeguard have been a favourite of mine since I first encountered them in 1974. Seen here leaving Guildford's Friary bus station on a town service soon after delivery in 1993 is K628 YPL. This bus, fitted with a Plaxton Pointer body, was their first Dennis Dart.

Entering the Safeguard fleet in 1996 was G89 KUB, a Mercedes-Benz 811D with an Optare StarRider body, purchased from Metroline. It is seen in North Street, Guildford, on 19 August 1998.

By the 1990s Safeguard had largely standardised on the Volvo B10M for its coach work, as shown here by G514 EFX, which was purchased from Excelsior of Bournemouth when barely six months old. It is seen here in 1994 on a private hire for Guildford Cathedral to the Royal Hospital, Chelsea.

Blue Saloon's Bristol LHs were still in evidence in the early 1990s, as shown here by former Western National VDV 107S, captured in Onslow Street, Guildford, in around 1993. This company did not survive the decade, being bought by London & Country in 1996.

The 1990s were a period of rapid expansion for the Tillingbourne company. Here, A889 FPM, a Bedford YMT with a Plaxton Bustler body, is seen entering Guildford along Millbrook, by the Yvonne Arnaud Theatre, while on service 22 from Dorking on 13 June 1990.

Tillingbourne started to brand their minibus operations under the 'Hobbit' name in 1989. Seen here in Guildford's Friary bus station on 14 March 1992 is B919 NPC, a relatively rare Bedford YMQ/S with a Lex Maxeta body, one of two they bought from Alder Valley South.

Tillingbourne invested heavily in updating their fleet during the 1990s, and bought some of the last Optare Vectas to be built. Seen here on Millbrook, Guildford, on 29 May 1999 is P108 OPX, working service 24 from Cranleigh.

Also photographed on 29 May 1999 was T591 CGT, one of two Dennis Dart SLFs with Plaxton Pointer 2 bodies that were bought by Surrey County Council and leased to Tillingbourne. Carrying a special Surrey Links livery, it is seen in Guildford Friary bus station on service 32 to Redhill.

Tillingbourne's rapid expansion during the 1990s saw it move into north-east Hampshire and Berkshire. It also saw the arrival of their first double-deckers in the shape of former London Country South West Volvo Citybuses with East Lancs bodies. Seen here on Station Hill, Reading, on 4 January 1999 is H678 GPF, working service 144 from Wokingham.

A short-lived operator in the Guildford area was Surrey Rider. Their former Alder Valley Leyland National TPE 150S is seen in Guildford's Friary bus station on 31 October 1999.

The West Sussex cathedral city of Chichester is the setting for Hants & Sussex AML 601H, a former London AEC Merlin with a MCW body, seen near the bus station in 1994.

A newer vehicle in the Hants & Sussex fleet was this Iveco 59.12 with an uncommon European Coach Conversions body, L625 RPX, bought new and seen near Chichester Cathedral in 1994.

Sussex Bus of Ford operated this former Ribble Iveco 59.12 with a Robin Hood body on a local service in Chichester, lettered as 'City Legs'. D624 BCK is photographed in 1994 outside the city's magnificent Norman cathedral.

Seen the same day in Chichester bus station is XSU 612. Formerly registered PWT 278W and numbered 2598 in the West Yorkshire fleet, this Leyland Leopard was rebodied in 1990 with this Willowbrook Warrior bus body, having previously carried a Willowbrook 003 coach body. This vehicle was eventually exported to Africa.

Excelsior of Bournemouth is an old established operator of coach tours and always had a very smart and up-to-date fleet. It has long been a provider of services on the National Express network. Here their vehicle A8 XCL, delivered new as P168 ALJ, is seen at Heathrow Airport during 1998. A Volvo B10M-62 with a Plaxton Premiere 350 body, it is working on NX service 205 to Bournemouth and Poole, one of a number of services serving London's airports and marketed under the 'Flightlink' brand.

Moving west, we come to the seaside town and former naval base of Weymouth and to Portland Bill, the home of Smiths of Portland, who started providing services around the Weymouth area in the mid-1920s. In the early 1990s Smiths were using former Bristol Omnibus Bristol REs on their service from Weymouth to Portland Bill. Here we see YHY 596J descending Portland Bill on its way back to Weymouth. The REs wore the livery of Western National, from whom they were bought in 1990. They survived until 1996.

At the other end of the route from Portland Bill we find YHY 586J waiting at the terminus, the King's Statue in Weymouth, on a sunny summer's day in 1995.

Cuff of Piddlehinton was another keen user of Bristol REs, operating six over the years, including three that originated with the Eastern Counties fleet. Seen here entering Yeovil bus station during 1998 on service 243 from Sturminster Newton is GCL 349N, a Bristol RELH6L with the usual ECW body. It was originally Eastern Counties RLE 746.

A major operator in the Yeovil area was Wake's of Sparkford. Pictured entering Yeovil bus station on 18 August 1998 is UYD 950W, a Bedford YMT with a Duple Dominant body purchased in 1988 from Osmond of Curry Rivel.

Another well-known operator in the Yeovil area was Safeway of South Petherton. Their bus operations are well known, but in this view we see two of their coach fleet on a private hire to Penzance during 1997. Both coaches are Leyland Tigers, with E565 YYA carrying a Duple 320 body and C744 JYA a relatively rare Willowbrook Crusader body. E565 YYA was destined to be exported to Zimbabwe.

The East Devon fleet of Gascoine, Sampford, included this Dennis Dart with UVG body, N428 FOW, which was purchased new in 1996. Seen leaving Tiverton bus station for Dulverton in 1996, this vehicle didn't stay long in Devon, moving to the Thames Transit fleet in Oxford after a year.

During the 1990s and early 2000s, Tally Ho of Kingsbridge operated a large number of former London Bristol LHs. With their 7-foot 6-inch-wide ECW bodies they were ideal for the narrow lanes of the South Hams in South Devon. Here we see KJD 419P, formerly London Transport BL19, leaving Kingsbridge for Plymouth.

Captured in Plymouth's Bretonside bus station on 26 May 1998 is A892 FRY from the fleet of Fry's of Tintagel on the north Cornwall coast. A Bedford YNT, its Plaxton Paramount 3200 Express body is complete with King Arthur emblazoned along the side.

Seen resting in Bretonside bus station, Plymouth, is D809 SGB from the fleet of Jennings of Bude on the north Cornwall coast. This Volvo B10M with a Plaxton Paramount 3500 III body joined the fleet in April 1993, staying until March 1998, when the business passed to Hookways of Meeth.

A more unusual coach to be found in an independent's fleet was the Bristol RELH. This example, IJI 5367, has a Plaxton Panorama Elite II body and originated with Greenslades, where it was registered UFJ 229J. By the summer of 1995, when this photograph was taken in Bretonside bus station, Plymouth, it had entered the local Plymouth-based fleet of Girlings, and had also acquired a sun visor.

Tavistock bus station is the setting for Ford's of Gunnislake YAF 872. This Duple Dominant-bodied Bedford YRQ was new to Jones of Newchurch as HVJ 146N, finding its way to rural Devon in May 1992 after spells with two other Welsh operators. It is seen awaiting departure on a local journey to Calstock.

Hambly's Coaches, from the small village of Pelynt, provided a local service around the popular town of Looe on Cornwall's south coast. Seen here working that service on 11 August 1998 is L329 LSC, a Mercedes-Benz 709D with a Dormobile body that originated in Scotland and was bought from Irvine of Law.

During the 1990s the fleet of Webbers of Blisland was to a large extent made up of second-hand Leyland Leopards. Seen here on Bay Tree Hill, Liskeard, on 18 August 1992 is KHE 878P, a Duple Dominant-bodied example purchased from Ranger of London in 1988.

Two Plaxton-bodied examples of Webbers fleet of Leyland Leopards are seen here at their depot in the village of Blisland, high up on Bodmin Moor. TUP 338K is an Elite Express II-bodied example that started life in the North East with Trimdon Motor Services, while GTA 807N carries a Panorama Elite III body and originated with Western National as their vehicle number 2426.

An operator who ceased trading during the 1990s was Willis of Bodmin. They had an interesting fleet that included this former Greater Manchester Bristol VRT with an ECW body, pictured at the depot in Bodmin in 1992, with Plaxton Supreme-bodied Bedford YMT LHW 504P behind. Happily, the VR is now preserved.

Captured in the picturesque village of Port Isaac is HAF 430N, a Duple Dominant-bodied Bedford YRT from the locally based firm of Prout. It is seen at the terminus awaiting departure to Wadebridge. The terminus is above the village as the streets of Port Isaac are too narrow for vehicles like this, as fans of the TV series *Doc Martin* will know!

The village of Par, between Lostwithiel and St Austell, is the home to Roselyn Coaches. Their standard double-decker throughout the 1980s and early 1990s was the AEC Regent V, including a number purchased from the AERE at Harwell. 241 AJB, fitted with a Park Royal body and dating from 1962, was one of these. It lasted with the company until 1996, being used on, and lettered for, a Park & Ride service in nearby Mevagissey. Seen here at the Middleway Depot in Par in 1995, it has since been preserved by the company.

When Roselyn withdrew their former AERE AEC Regents Vs they retained the AJB registration numbers and transferred them to members of their coach fleet. The first recipient of the number 244AJB was this AEC Reliance with a Plaxton Supreme body, originally registered MUN 942R and purchased from Geen of South Molton in 1980. It is seen here in Truro's Lemon Street coach park in 1995.

Roselyn's TMW 997S, formerly Green Line coach RB57 and registered VPH 57S, found its way to Cornwall via MC Travel of Melksham in Wiltshire. Seen outside the Royal Talbot Hotel in Lostwithiel on its way to Plymouth, it is an AEC Reliance with a Duple Dominant II Express body.

The major operator in the cathedral city of Truro, after Western National, was undoubtedly Truronian. Caught in Truro's Lemon Street coach park on 17 February 1992 was RPH 105L, an ECW-bodied Bristol LHS6L that came to Truronian from Bristol Omnibus, although it originated with London Country.

Truronian's double-decker fleet was interesting and varied at this time in the early 1990s. Here we see RNA 220J, a former Greater Manchester Daimler Fleetline with a Park Royal body to the design, dubbed the 'Mancunian'. It is seen on Lemon Quay, Truro, in 1993.

Leyland Atlantean SFS 159V was an interesting vehicle, starting life in 1970 as a test rig for the Atlantean AN68 chassis. Fitted with an Alexander body, it wasn't registered until 1980, when it passed to Rennie of Dunfermline. Truronian purchased it in October 1983 and it is seen here on Lemon Quay, Truro, on 10 August 1992.

By the mid-1990s Truronian had standardised on the Dennis Dart with Plaxton Pointer bodies for its single-deckers. One of the second batch of Darts, but the first of the Dart SLF, was P455 SCV, seen here in St Agnes in March 1997.

An unusual vehicle in the Truronian fleet was H920 XYN, a Renault G10 with a Wadham Stringer Vanguard body bought from the Royal Borough of Kensington and Chelsea in 1986. It is seen here in Truro on 6 August 1998.

Hopley's Coaches of Mount Hawke near St Agnes still operate into Truro with a service from Porthtowan. This 1995 view shows VCU 889Y, a Bedford YNT with a Plaxton Paramount 3200 Express body on Lemon Quay starting out on its return run.

In 1997 Hopley's placed P87 SAF in service, a Volvo B10B with Wright Endurance body. It is pictured here in Truro on 6 August 1998. This vehicle passed to Delaine, Bourne, in 2003 and has since been preserved in their livery.

Palmer of Blackwater, trading as Wheal Briton, operated a service to Truro from their home village, normally using one of their fleet of AEC coaches. An unusual vehicle in their fleet was JIL 9409. A former RAF bus used for transporting RAF bands to engagements, this 1979 Marshall-bodied AEC Reliance found its way to Palmer after a period with Chiltern Queens of Woodcote. It was photographed in a very wet Truro in 1995.

NIW 3649 is an AEC Reliance, new to Central of Rippondon as DCX 664S. Reregistered in 1997, its Plaxton Supreme IV body was rejuvenated with new bus seats. It was captured in Truro on 6 August 1998.

The south-west of England has long been a popular destination for coach holidays, and most if not all of the big names of coaching would be found there, especially during the summer months. One example of this is Shearings, whose bright blue coaches were a familiar sight on my frequent trips to Cornwall. Here, Scania K93CRB J271 NNC, fitted with a Plaxton Premiere 320 body, is seen on Lemon Quay, Truro, on 10 August 1992.

Another visitor to Cornwall's county town, this time on 25 May 1998, was H242 AFV – a DAF MB230 with a Van Hool Alizee body from the fleet of Robinsons of Great Harwood.

Gill & Munden of Wadebridge was another independent operator to operate services into Truro. LUA 282V, a former Wallace Arnold Leyland Leopard with a Plaxton Supreme IV body, is caught awaiting time in Truro before departing for Newquay. Independent operators in Truro at this time used the coach park on Lemon Quay as their terminus as the bus station was used solely by Western National. Nowadays all operators use the new bus station built on the site of this coach park.

A smaller company running coach holidays to Cornwall was Slack of Matlock in Derbyshire. R411 YWJ, their Dennis Javelin with a Plaxton Premiere 320 body, was caught on Lemon Quay in Truro on 25 May 1998.

Thomas of Relubbus traded as Brookside Travel. In service with them in 1993 was HJT 39N, a former Hants & Dorset Bristol LH with an ECW body that found its way to deepest Cornwall after spending time with Holladay of Clyst Honiton in Devon and Trimdon Motor Services in the North East. It is seen leaving Penzance bus station, situated right by the sea, for Goldsithney.

A popular destination for holidaymakers in Cornwall is St Ives. All the visiting coaches have to park in the coach park overlooking the town and the harbour, and their passengers either walk (it's a tough walk back!) or use the local minibus service down into the town. Seen in the coach park, with its panoramic view, in the summer of 1996 is Harry Shaw's L42 VRW, a Volvo B10M with a Plaxton Premiere 320 body.

Filers of Barnstaple operate a number of bus services across North Devon, as well as a fleet of coaches engaged on UK and Continental tours. A member of their bus fleet in the summer of 1995 was G899 MNS, a Volvo B10M-56 with a Plaxton Derwent body that originated with Whitelaw of Stonehouse and arrived with Filer's in 1994 by way of Turner of Bristol. It is seen here in the coach park above the picturesque village of Clovelly.

Bakers of Weston-super-Mare have long had a major presence in Somerset, operating an extensive fleet of coaches for tours and private hires plus a number of buses for school contract work. Parked at the depot in Weston on 4 July 1990 was JOV 686P, a Bristol VRTSL with unusual MCW bodywork that originated with West Midlands PTE as its 4686. Next to it is FTO 554V, a Bedford YMT with a Plaxton Supreme IV Express body, one of a number purchased from Barton of Chilwell.

Also in Weston on 4 July 1990 was one of the smaller members of Baker's fleet, E521 TOV. A Carlyle-bodied Iveco Daily, it remained in the fleet until 1994.

Streamline of Bath operated this Mercedes-Benz 811D with a Marshall body on local services around Bath. Pictured in Manvers Street in 1996, M45 BEG is one of four such vehicles purchased in 1994.

Seen the same day, also in Manvers Street, is N28 FWU, a DAF SB220 with Hungarian Ikarus bodywork. Seen here on a service to the university, it is passing a Ford Transit minibus of local coach operator Arleen of Peasedown St John, an operator that is happily still with us.

Bristol VRs became popular choices with independent operators as they became available upon withdrawal by major operators, with some companies building up sizable fleets of them. One such company was Ashby of Gloucester, who traded as Circle-Line and operated a total of over thirty of these vehicles. LEU 266P, with the usual ECW bodywork, was acquired from Bristol Omnibus in late 1990, where it was numbered 5058. It survived in the fleet until 1996, when it was scrapped. It is seen here working a Park & Ride service in Cheltenham.

Another operator to appreciate the Bristol VR was James of Sherston, near Malmesbury in Wiltshire. They purchased GRF 702V (former PMT 702) in 1993 from Somerbus of Paulton. It is seen here in Swindon bus station. It passed to Coombs of Weston-super-Mare in early 1996.

My visits to Wales during the 1990s were very rare. However, 2 September 1999 found me in Newport, where I photographed Dennis Dart SLF R421 AOR from the fleet of Williams of Crosskeys in the bus station. Williams purchased this example, fitted with the less common UVG Urbanstar body, in 1998.

Trips to the English/Welsh border territory around Hereford did become more common during the 1990s, with opportunities to observe and photograph firms such as the well-known Yeoman company. Seen in Hereford Country bus station having arrived on a 453 journey from Fownhope is MKP 181W. A Bedford YMT with a high-capacity Wadham Stringer Vanguard body, this vehicle originated with Maidstone Borough Council – an unusual choice for a municipal company – and found its way to Hereford in late 1994 via Metrobus of Orpington and Cave of Shirley. It remained in the fleet for around two years before moving on to nearby Primrose of Leominster.

A more common vehicle in the Yeoman fleet was JVJ 439P, a Bedford YRQ, fitted this time with a more usual Duple Dominant body. Photographed the same day as the previous picture, this vehicle was new to the company in 1975, surviving until 1998. It is seen in Hereford on a service to Broad Oak.

Also seen in Hereford, on a 449 service to Madley, is FCY 295W. This is a former South Wales Transport Bedford YMQ (again with a Duple Dominant body) that was purchased in 1994, after a period of time working in Hertfordshire. It stayed with Yeoman for five years. Behind it is Bedford YMT EFO 300W.

Seen here entering Wolverhampton bus station is THX 151S, a 10.3-metre Leyland National from the fleet of Chase Coaches of Chasetown. A former London Buses vehicle, it was purchased in 1990 and is seen on a 1994 trip to the West Midlands. Leyland Nationals were becoming popular purchases for independent operators during the 1990s.

Another operator in Wolverhampton that day was Glen Stuart of Willenhall, whose WRN 14R is seen entering the bus station. This former Burnley & Pendle Leyland Leopard PSU4 was fitted with the stylish Alexander Y type body and found its way to Stuart's fleet by way of Ogden of Haydock on Merseyside.

The main purpose of the trip to the West Midlands had been to photograph the vehicles of Stevenson's of Uttoxeter, who were by now the largest independent operator in the country. Seen here entering Wolverhampton bus station is J31 SFA. It is a comparatively rare Leyland Swift with a Wright Handybus body.

Citybus in Belfast were the only operator to acquire Leyland Lynxes with bodywork other than Leyland. In 1986 they purchased seven vehicles with bodies built by Alexander Belfast, classified as the N type. In 1992 the entire batch passed to Stevenson's and HXI 3008 is seen here in Burton-on-Trent on a service to Swadlincote.

Seen in Burton-on-Trent the same day is L94 HRF, an Optare Spectra on a DAF DB250 chassis, one of two purchased in late 1993. It is working to Birmingham on Stevenson's trunk 112 service.

Stevenson's also developed a liking for MCW Metrobuses, purchasing a number from several different sources, including South Yorkshire PTE, West Midlands PTE and West Yorkshire PTE, as well as a couple of former demonstrators. One of the former West Yorkshire examples, fitted with an Alexander RH body, is seen here in Burton-on-Trent, bound for Winshill. Stevenson's was purchased by British Bus in 1994 and subsequently became part of the Arriva Group.

Flights of Birmingham were a long-established operator of coach tours. Additionally they operated services from Birmingham to Heathrow and Gatwick. Seen here at Heathrow Airport on 12 April 1999, S295 WOA, then only around three months old, is a Volvo B10M-62 with a Plaxton Premiere 350 body.

A couple of opportunities came my way during 1994 to photograph vehicles in the Manchester area. Deregulation in the late 1980s had brought a plethora of operators on to the streets of Manchester, adding colour and variety. An example was Wall of Sharston, who operated a large fleet of second-hand double-deckers. Seen here in Manchester Piccadilly is HJB 460W, an ECW-bodied Bristol VRT that originated with my then local bus company Alder Valley. Walls was to cease trading before the end of the decade.

Walls also purchased a number of new DAF SB220s with Optare Delta bodies. G316 YHJ is seen here, again in Manchester Piccadilly, bound for Gatley in April 1994.

Seen here in April 1994 near, I believe, the Free Trade Hall in Manchester – a concert hall I was once fortunate enough to play in – is Stuart's of Dukinfield JKW 335W, a Leyland Atlantean with uncommon Marshall bodywork that originated with South Yorkshire PTE. Stuart's purchased this vehicle from A1 Service of Ardrossan in 1994, keeping it until 1997.

Manchester Piccadilly is the venue for Stuart's former West Midlands PTE Leyland Fleetline SDA 613S, fitted with Park Royal bodywork.

A new operator to be found on the streets of Manchester in 1994 was South Manchester Transport, operating from a base in Hyde. One of their early acquisitions was PKA 724S, a Leyland Atlantean with a MCW body purchased from nearby Merseyside PTE. South Manchester lasted a bare three years, ceasing trading in 1997.

An old established operator in Manchester is Maynes of Clayton, running services mostly between Manchester and Ashton-under-Lyne. A relatively rare vehicle to join their fleet in 1991 was A44 YWJ, one of four Marshall-bodied Dennis Falcon HCs purchased from Chesterfield that year. It is seen here in Manchester Piccadilly in October 1994, bound for Arndale on service 120.

Scanias, both double- and single-deckers, became very popular with Maynes, with both new and second-hand examples being added to the fleet. Seen in Piccadilly at the same time as the Dennis Falcon above was G117 SBA, a Scania N113DRB with a Northern Counties body purchased new in early 1990. It is seen here working the 235 service to Ashton-under-Lyne.

A well-known coach operator that branched out into bus operation at deregulation was Shearings, who used a fleet of second-hand Leyland Nationals before buying brand-new Leyland Lynxes, plus Leyland Tigers and Volvo B10Ms, fitted with Alexander (Belfast) bodies. These operations were sold to Timeline in the early 1990s. Here, one of the Leyland Tigers, G66 RND, is seen crossing the tram tracks in Manchester Piccadilly in 1994.

Another Manchester coach operator to branch out into local bus operation after deregulation was Finglands, who operated to the south of the city using a fleet of second-hand double-deckers. In 1992 they were taken over by the privatised East Yorkshire company. Here, former Harrow Buses MCW Metrobus Mk 2 E480 UOF is seen parked in Manchester Piccadilly in October 1994.

Former Greater Manchester vehicles featured in Finglands fleet quite prominently. Entering Manchester Piccadilly in October 1994 on service 41, one of the Wilmslow Road group of routes, is Northern Counties-bodied Leyland Atlantean JDB 121N.

Citibus of Chadderton was another operator who took advantage of deregulation to branch into bus operations. By the early 1990s the fleet had a large number of Leyland Atlanteans, many originating with South Yorkshire Transport. Here, Roe-bodied VET 615S is seen working service 161 in October 1994.

Another former South Yorkshire Roe-bodied Atlantean photographed in October 1994 was XWG 638T, seen here crossing the tram tracks in Manchester Piccadilly. Citibus was taken over by Greater Manchester North in 1995, joining the First Group family the following year.

Bullock of Cheadle was another operator who diversified into bus operation at deregulation. It also took advantage of London's premature disposal of its DMS class Fleetlines. Here, OJD 249R (former London DMS 2249), a Leyland Fleetline to the special B20 specification and carrying an MCW body, is seen crossing the tram tracks in Manchester Piccadilly on its way to Parrswood in 1994.

Bullocks maintained quite a varied bus fleet, as shown here by CKS 385X, a MCW Metrobus with an Alexander body that originated with Alexander Midland as their MRM5. It found its way to Manchester via Kelvin Scottish and BTS of Borehamwood. It is also operating on the service to Parrswood.

Moving north from Manchester we come to the city of Preston, and the vehicles of well-known independent J. Fishwick & Sons. Caught in Preston bus station while laying over on a 109 working to Chorley is Leyland Lynx Mk 2 J7 JFS.

Buses carrying Q registrations are rare. Seen entering Burnley bus station in 1994, Border Buses Q364 FVT had an interesting life, having carried three different bodies during its career. Starting life as LJX 817H, this Leyland Leopard was delivered new to Hebble, carrying a Plaxton Panorama Elite body. In 1985 it was rebodied with a Duple body and reregistered Q364 FVT, and it was in this guise it passed to Cartmell of Burnley (trading as Border Buses) in 1989. In 1992 it was rebodied again with this Willowbrook Warrior bus body.

The chance of a long weekend in the North East in 1994 found me in the Northumberland town of Hexham, between Carlisle and Newcastle, which is famous for its beautiful abbey. Seen here in the bus station is SPW 101R, a former Eastern Counties Leyland Leopard with a Duple Dominant I Express body of Rochester & Marshall. Now reseated with bus seats, it is seen working on a Hexham town service.

Another Duple-bodied Leyland Leopard in the Rochester & Marshall fleet was WCK 131V, although this time fitted with a Dominant II Express body, but also reseated with bus seats. Seen outside the bus station, this vehicle is also engaged on town service work.

Operating on Tyneside, Classic Coaches of Annfield Plain had ANC 923T, a former Greater Manchester Park Royal-bodied Leyland Atlantean, working on service 21 into Newcastle. It is seen during that 1994 visit in Market Street East, Newcastle.

A well-known name from the far North East visiting the far South West. OK Travel of Bishop Auckland sent their Bova Futura A504 KFP to Cornwall in August 1991. It is seen here in Truro.

The OK fleet of over 200 vehicles was an interesting one, as the following selection of photographs will show – all taken on that 1994 trip. Here, former South Yorkshire Transport Alexander-bodied Leyland Atlantean CWG 730V is seen at Eldon Square, Newcastle, bound for Whickham.

Seen the same day as the Atlantean is L401 FVN, a Plaxton Pointer-bodied Volvo B6. It is leaving Eldon Square, Newcastle, for Birtley on service 727.

Working the same route as the Volvo that day was former Rhymney Valley East Lancs-bodied Leyland Leopard LBO 83X, seen here approaching Eldon Square.

Seen here in Newcastle city centre is former Eastern Counties MCL 933P, a Leyland Leopard with an Alexander T type body, now fitted with bus seats in lieu of the coach seats originally carried. It is being pursued by two Go-Ahead Optare Metroriders – a sign of things to come?

On the same service as MCL was PKG 724R, a Leyland Leopard with a Duple Dominant I Express body, again now fitted with bus seats. Originally in the National Welsh fleet, it is seen here near Newcastle Central station.

Pictured in Bishop Auckland bus station during 1994 is GMS 279S (former Alexander Midland MPE 279). Bearing the classic Scottish combination of a Leyland Leopard chassis and Alexander Y type body, it is seen awaiting departure for Darlington.

Leaving Bishop Auckland bus station for Evenwood, the site of OK's original garage, is XUP 348L, a Leyland Atlantean with a Northern Counties body that was new to the company in 1973.

In company with a number of United Automobile Leylands – including a former Trimdon Motor Services Duple-bodied Leyland Tiger bus – is OK's K108 YVN, a Northern Counties-bodied Leyland Olympian, bound for Newcastle. This was quite possibly one of the last Olympians to be badged as a Leyland as the Volvo name began appearing on them around this time.

TAJ 295R (former London Transport BL93) was originally registered OJD 93R. These 30-foot-long ECW-bodied Bristol LHs were only 7 feet 6 inches wide. This example is seen leaving Bishop Auckland bus station on a local service.

The roots of Eden Bus services date back to 1927, when the company was founded as Summerson Brothers. Eden became the name of the company in 1976. RJI 5344 started life as KJD 527P, numbered LS27 in the London Transport fleet. Converted to single door with dual-purpose seating in 1986, it joined Eden Bus services in 1994 and is seen later that year leaving Bishop Auckland bus station for Darlington.

Bond of Willington in County Durham bought PRH 248G in 1990 from Hull Corporation. A Roe-bodied Leyland Atlantean, it is seen here leaving Bishop Auckland bus station for its home village of Willington in 1994.

Leyland Leopard BVP 796V started life with Midland Red. By the middle of 1990 it had found its way to Bob Smith Travel of Langley Park in County Durham, who replaced its original Willowbrook 003 coach body with this somewhat boxy Willowbrook Warrior bus body. It is seen working service 754 into Durham in 1994.

Leyland National CBO 29V started life with Taff-Ely in Caerphilly before passing to National Welsh. In 1990 it moved to the North East to join the fleet of Robson of Thornaby. It is seen in Middlesbrough.

Delta of Stockton became keen users of Bristol REs during the late 1980s and early 1990s, operating a large number mostly with ECW bodies. IIL 1839 was originally registered NWU 321M and was numbered 1396 in the West Yorkshire fleet. It found its way to Delta from the North Devon company in 1986 and is seen here in Middlesbrough during 1994.

UEL 566J started life with Hants & Dorset before joining the Wilts & Dorset fleet when the former company was split. It migrated to Delta via Wright of Millport in 1986 and survived until 1995. Again, it is seen in Middlesbrough in 1994.

Unlike UEL, XLJ 729K was always a Wilts & Dorset vehicle, spending a lot of its life in Salisbury before joining Delta in 1991, where it survived until 1995.

The National Holidays name was acquired by the Godfrey Burley Group when East Yorkshire Travel was separated from East Yorkshire Motor Services. Starting life in the fleet of Tyne & Wear PTE as part of their Armstrong Galley fleet, KSU 454 was originally registered B104 DVK. A Leyland Tiger with a Van Hool Alizee body, it is seen here on 4 August 1998 in Truro.

Seen at York station in October 1993, EGR 707S was delivered new to Northern General as their 7007 in 1978. A Leyland Leopard with a Plaxton Supreme Express body, it was purchased by Stephenson's of Easingwold in 1991, who modified it by fitting the Supreme IV front panel.

One of the most well-known names in the independent sector must have undoubtedly been Wallace Arnold, whose coaches were a familiar sight across the whole country. Allocated to their Devon fleet was CSU 937, a short Leyland Leopard delivered in 1977 with a Duple body as WUG 127S and rebodied in 1987 with this Plaxton Paramount body. It was an ideal vehicle for use on the narrow Dartmoor lanes. Happily this vehicle survives in preservation.

Captured resting in Truro in the summer of 1993 while awaiting the return of its passengers, K760 FYG was a Volvo B10M with Plaxton Premiere 320 bodywork. During the 1990s, the Volvo B10M was the vehicle of choice for Wallace Arnold, with bodywork being shared between Plaxton, Jonckheere and Van Hool.

Seen entering Sheffield's Pond Street bus station to pick up passengers for a tour to Sandown on the Isle of Wight is J735 CWT, a Wallace Arnold Volvo, this time carrying Plaxton Excalibur bodywork.

A more unusual vehicle in an independent fleet was XCK 219R, a Willowbrook 008 Spacecar-bodied Leyland Leopard PSU5, originally in the fleet of National Travel West, named *Kirk* after the character from *Star Trek*. It joined the fleet of Yorkshire Terrier in 1989, and is seen here in Sheffield on 2 April 1990 working an X29 service to Killamarsh. It had been withdrawn by the end of the year.

Another uncommon vehicle in the Yorkshire Terrier fleet was D91 ALX, an East Lancs-bodied Scania K112CRB. This vehicle started life with British Airways at Heathrow Airport before moving to Yorkshire in 1992. It is seen entering Sheffield bus station in September 1993.

Another independent operator who developed a liking for Bristol REs was Sheldon in North Anston. Here, OCK 367K – a RESL with an ECW body – is seen entering Dinnington bus station on 11 September 1993, bound for Worksop. Starting life as Ribble 367, it arrived with Sheldon via Blackburn Transport. Happily this RE survives in preservation.

Sheffield during the 1990s was something of a hotbed of competition between bus operators. One of the operators was Sheffield Omnibus, who came into being in 1990, lasting until 1996. During their short existence they built up a sizable fleet of Leyland Atlanteans, among other types, all smartly turned out in this blue and cream livery. Seen here entering Sheffield bus station on service 21 to Stocksbridge is East Lancs-bodied Atlantean OYJ 65R, now numbered 1065 in the Sheffield Omnibus fleet. It migrated to South Yorkshire from the south coast, having served with Brighton Corporation. This vehicle ended its days in Ireland.

Working to the large shopping centre at Meadowhall is BFR 304R, a long-wheelbase Atlantean with East Lancs body that started life as Blackpool Corporation 304, and now numbered 1104 in the Sheffield Omnibus fleet. This bus moved to Essex in 1994 and served with Abridge of Hadleigh.

An interesting Atlantean in the Sheffield Omnibus fleet was IIL 2501. Starting life registered LJA 645P and carrying a Northern Counties double-deck body, it was originally 7645 in the Greater Manchester fleet. Passing to Hyndburn (Accrington) in 1988, it came to Sheffield in 1991 and received this single-deck East Lancs body in 1992. Bound for Stocksbridge in this 1993 view, it is seen outside Sheffield station.

A more usual single-decker in the Sheffield Omnibus fleet was this Leyland National 2, DMS 18V. Beginning its career with Alexander Midland as their MPN 18, by the time it reached Sheffield Omnibus it had served with a total of six operators before finishing its days as a driver trainer with Yorkshire Traction, who bought the company in 1995.

Sheafline was set up by a group of drivers made redundant by South Yorkshire Transport. A more unusual vehicle in the predominantly Leyland National fleet was E101 VWA, one of two Neoplan N416s they operated. Starting life as demonstrator, it is seen here in Sheffield bus station on 3 April 1990.

Caught in Pinstone Street, Sheffield, on 2 April 1990 is XJA 507L, a Park Royal-bodied Leyland Atlantean that was new as SELNEC 7116 and bought by Sheafline in 1988. It was withdrawn a month after this photograph was taken.

Seen in Commercial Street, Sheffield, on 3 April 1990, this smartly turned out 10.3-metre Leyland National was new to the Burnley, Colne & Nelson fleet.

Sheffield United Tours was originally a well-known operator of tours and express services. Resurrected under the name SUT, it began competing on the streets of Sheffield. They operated a mixed fleet, including a number of former Edinburgh Leyland Atlanteans, such as WFS 281K, seen in Pond Street on 2 April 1990.

Seen the same day, this time at Sheffield bus station, is HNL 160N, a former Tyne & Wear Leyland National.

Barnsley & District led a short life. Formed in 1990, it built up a fleet of Leyland Nationals such as SGR 551R, a former Northern General vehicle seen here in Sheffield. This firm became part of the Yorkshire Traction group in 1994.

Andrews of Sheffield started operations as a PSV driving school. With the advent of deregulation they entered the bus market, favouring Daimler Fleetlines in a smart blue and yellow livery. Here, CWE 797N – an ECW-bodied example formerly with South Yorkshire – is seen in Pond Street, Sheffield, on 3 April 1990.

Captured on 2 April 1990 in Orchard Lane is DMS lookalike OKW 515R, a MCW-bodied vehicle that was again originally in the South Yorkshire fleet.

A former Greater Manchester example was YNA 338M, a Northern Counties-bodied vehicle. It is seen here in Pond Street on 3 April 1990.

A company much loved by enthusiasts because of their enthusiasm for Bristol REs was Northern Bus of Anston. Seen here in Sheffield is NKG 245M, a Bristol RESL with an ECW body that was originally in the Gelligaer fleet in South Wales. This vehicle passed to Northern in 1989, as is seen here on 2 April 1990.

Seen at Sheffield bus station on 11 September 1993 is a particular favourite of mine: RHT 141G, a RELL6L. Joining Northern Bus in 1992, it was delivered new to Bristol Omnibus at Wells Garage, my home depot, and passed to Badgerline, receiving their livery before being repainted into its original Bristol livery of Tilling Green, still based in Wells. It originally carried a T type destination display that was replaced with this side-by-side display after accident damage. Sadly, RHT was scrapped in 1995.

The 12-metre Bristol REMH was never a common variant of the RE chassis. Eastern Scottish and Western SMT bought them with Alexander M type bodies for the Scotland to London services, and very stylish they were, especially in the Eastern Scottish livery of black and yellow. The only English company to use the REMH was United Automobile, who bought thirty-five examples with Plaxton Panorama Elite II and Elite III bodies. One of the latter was SHN 111L, which found its way to Northern Bus via PAB Transport of Dublin. It is seen here entering Dinnington bus station while en route to Sheffield on service X60 on 11 September 1993.

Former Ribble OCK 350K, a Bristol RESL6L, was painted in this bright red livery as the 'Hillsborough Bus'. Seen here entering Sheffield bus station on 11 September 1993, this vehicle spent some time in Northern Ireland with Citybus.

Northern Bus also built up a fleet of Bristol VRs, as shown here by former Yorkshire Traction XAK 908T, painted as the 'Bradfield Bus'. It is seen here at Dinnington bus station on 11 September 1993.

An older Bristol VR with Northern Bus was XMO 541H. New to Thames Valley, I remember photographing this vehicle in Reading during its days with Alder Valley. It passed to Northern Bus in late 1992, gaining the name *Constable Knapweed* after the character in the childrens' TV series *The Herbs*. It is seen at Dinnington bus station on 11 September 1993.

Photographed on 3 April 1990 at Sheffield bus station, RPH 106L is a Bristol LHS6L with an ECW body. It was new to London Country, joining Northern Bus in 1988.

Caught on a holiday tour to Cornwall, former Shearings YXI 9258 is a Volvo B10M with Van Hool Alizee body. Originally registered F751 ENE, it passed to Skills of Nottingham in 1996 and was seen in St Ives during summer 1997. The minibuses in the background are to take coach passengers down to the town and the harbour.

Dunn-Line of Nottingham built up a sizable bus and coach fleet during the 1990s. Seen here at the Brighton Coach Rally in April 1999 is A3 BOB, a recently delivered Scania with an Irizar Century body.

Also attending the Brighton Coach Rally that year was Dunn-Line's brand-new T32 CNN, a Jonckheere Monaco-bodied Volvo B12T fitted out to a high specification, including ski boxes for trips to the Alps.

This MAN with a Noge Catalan body belonging to Yorks of Cogenhoe in Northamptonshire was only around three months old when photographed in Truro on 4 August 1998. MAN was another manufacturer beginning to make its presence felt in the UK during the 1990s.

The Premier Travel fleet in the 1990s included this former Wallace Arnold Volvo B10M with a Plaxton Paramount 3500 III body. Purchased in 1991, E904 UNW is seen here passing through Oxford while bound for Cambridge on a National Express working in 1993.

Holder of Charlton-on-Otmoor near Bicester operated this Plaxton Paramount 3500 II-bodied Leyland Tiger from 1993 to 1998. Originally registered B216 NDG in the Cheltenham & Gloucester fleet, LIL 2665 is seen on a private hire in Oxford in 1996.

Cambridge Coach Services were responsible for operating services from Cambridge to the London airports. Here, Volvo B10M N312 VAV, fitted with a Plaxton Premiere 350 body, is seen at Heathrow Airport on 27 August 1999.

An East Anglian firm that started operating on behalf of National Express was Charter Coach of Great Oakley in Essex. KIB 6991 was caught in Victoria coach station on 10 February 1990 while operating service 082. This Leyland Leopard began life with a Willowbrook 003 body in the Eastern Counties fleet, registered OEX 795W. It joined Charter Coach in 1986 and received this relatively rare Willowbrook Crusader body in 1988. Just creeping into the shot next to KIB is a Trathens Neoplan double-deck coach on a Plymouth service.

Flitwick, south of Bedford, was the home of Buffalo Bus. Seen here at Watford Junction station in 1993 is K448 XPA, a Plaxton Pointer-bodied Dennis Dart on a service to London Colney, with a Carlyle-bodied Dart of Luton & District behind.

Buffalo bought this former Nottingham Northern Counties-bodied Leyland Olympian in 1990. This 1994 photograph of A699 EAU at Milton Keynes bus station clearly shows the narrower entrance door specified by Nottingham.

Seen in St Peter's Street, St Albans, on 30 July 1992 is Volvo B10M HIL 7467. This coach was delivered new to Wallace Arnold as FUA 387Y, and fitted with a Plaxton Paramount 3200 body. Sold to Summerfield of Southampton, its original body was destroyed by fire and it passed to Buffalo, who fitted this East Lancs body.

Also seen on 30 July 1992 in St Peter's Street, St Albans, was Seamarks of Westoning H46 UUA, an Optare Vecta with MAN chassis that was formerly a demonstrator for Optare. It is seen on a service from Borehamwood.

University Bus of Hatfield was a company set up by the University of Hertfordshire primarily to provide student transport around the various campuses. However, their services were also available to the general public. In 1994 they purchased four American-built Blue Bird buses, a manufacturer more commonly associated with specialist school buses. M49 HUT is seen in St Peter's Street, St Albans, on 13 April 1999.

A more familiar type of vehicle in the University Bus fleet is R654 VBM, a Wright Crusader-bodied Dennis Dart SLF, also seen on 13 April 1999, this time at Watford Junction station.

Another operator working into Watford Junction was Red Rose of Weston Turnville in Berkshire. Their N784 JBM, a Mercedes-Benz 711D with an UVG body, is seen on the stands in the bus station on a local service on 13 April 1999.

Mott of Stoke Mandeville in Buckinghamshire traded as Yellow Bus for their stage services. They purchased MUS 152P, a Duple Dominant-bodied Leyland Leopard new to Graham of Paisley, from Williams of Cross Keys in 1993. It is seen here at Reading station in 1994.

Seen at the same place some five years later, on 4 January 1999, OWG 368X started life with Wilson of Stainforth in South Yorkshire. A Leyland Leopard with a Plaxton Bustler body, it joined Mott's Yellow Bus fleet in 1991, staying with the firm until 2003.

Chiltern Queens of Woodcote in Oxfordshire were still working regular services into Reading during the 1990s. Optare StarRider F986 TTF was purchased from Lee & Back of Caversham in 1991 and is seen here at Reading station in 1997 wearing Chiltern Queens' coach livery, but working on a service back to its home village.

Also smartly painted in the coach livery was Chiltern Queens LUA 244V, a Volvo B58 with a Plaxton Supreme IV body that originated with Wallace Arnold and reached the company via Parry of Leominster. It is seen on a private hire at Reading station on 9 June 1990.

Chiltern Queens has purchased a number of vehicles from City of Oxford Motor Services over the years. YFC 18V, a Leyland Leopard with a Duple Dominant II Express body, originally operated on the Oxford to London services, but is seen here in Chiltern Queens' bus livery at Reading station in 1997 while awaiting departure to the village of Peppard, a short distance north of Reading.

January 1998 saw Tellings Golden Miller of Byfleet take over operation of service 235 from Sunbury to Brentford. Seen just over a year later, on 20 February 1999, is Plaxton Pointer-bodied Dennis Dart SLF R512 SJM, which is awaiting departure from Sunbury Cross.

Another Dennis Dart SLF with Tellings Golden Miller, this time with a Plaxton Pointer 2 body, was S518 TCF, seen here in Esher High Street on 9 March 1999 heading for Woking on service 471 from Kingston.

Tellings Golden Miller also ran a very smart coach fleet. Here, Plaxton Premiere 320-bodied Volvo B10M N40 TGM is seen on 27 August 1999 at Heathrow Airport.

Capital of West Drayton operated around Heathrow Airport on services such as crew transfers. The orange light mounted above the windscreen of R956 RCH, a short Plaxton Premiere-bodied Volvo B10M, signifies that it could operate airside at the airport. It is seen at Heathrow on 31 May 1999.

Another short Volvo B10M from the Capital fleet, this time with a Plaxton Paramount body, is J332 LLK, caught on 27 August 1999.

Capital also operated some local bus services. Here we see Optare Excel R993 EWU at Heathrow while operating a service to Uxbridge station on 9 March 1999.

London was a colourful place in the 1990s as a result of the changes to London bus operations. Panatlas won the contract for operation of service 107 to New Barnet. Seen in New Barnet on 30 July 1992 is G755 UYT, a Northern Counties-bodied Leyland Olympian.

Capital Citybus started operations in December 1990 when the London bus operations of Ensignbus were purchased by the Hong Kong-based CNT Group. Adopting a yellow livery that included Chinese characters, they built up a fleet of both new and second-hand vehicles. Here, former Southampton East Lancs-bodied Dennis Dominator F292 PTP is seen at Walthamstow bus station, departing for Stratford.

During 1995 Capital Citybus operated service ELX between Aldgate and New Cross Gate on behalf of London Underground. Seen here at Aldgate while wearing the special orange and white livery is CHF 347X, a Dennis Dominator with an Alexander body new to Merseyside PTE.

A trip to North London on 30 July 1992 to photograph some of the franchised operations found J613 HMF, a Capital Citybus Mercedes-Benz 811D with a Plaxton Beaver body, at Southgate station.

Grey-Green was the first independent operator to gain a route that penetrated Central London; namely, the 24 from Chalk Farm to Pimlico. Seen here in Trafalgar Square on 29 February 1992 is their Volvo Citybus G147 TYT, fitted with Alexander bodywork.

A second-hand member of the Grey-Green fleet is EWF 460V, a former South Yorkshire Metrobus seen at Southgate on 30 July 1992, bound for Winchmore Hill.

Seen at Brent Cross on 30 July 1992 is H918 XYT, an East Lancs-bodied Volvo B10M. Grey-Green also rebodied a number of their coach fleet with East Lancs bus bodies.

I always found Metrobus, with its origins in Tillingbourne, an interesting company, little knowing that in the late 2000s it would become my local operator. Former West Riding Leyland Olympian XWY 476X, one of a pair Metrobus bought in 1987, is seen outside Fairfield Halls, Croydon, on service 356 to Biggin Hill in 1995.

Seen on the same day, in the same place and on the same service is F166 SMT, a Leyland Lynx purchased by Metrobus from Miller of Foxton in 1991.

T313 SMV, a Dennis Dart SLF with a Plaxton Pointer 2 body, is seen here in Bromley working service 146 to Downe on 28 October 1999.

Metrobus Optare Excel P508 OUG, seen on Elmfield Road, Bromley, on 28 October 1999, heading for Orpington, was among the first low-floor vehicles delivered to Metrobus. This batch of ten vehicles were the only Excels bought by Metrobus.

The Olympian became the Metrobus standard double-decker throughout the 1990s. Here, S863 DGX, a Volvo with a Northern Counties Palatine I body, is seen in Bromley on service 261 to Lewisham on 28 October 1999.

Seen in Canterbury bus station having just arrived from Hythe in summer 1993, Leyland Lynx F608 WBV began life as a demonstrator for Leyland before passing to Westbus in 1990.

Parked between two East Kent Bristol VRs, Leyland National KRE 279P passed to Poynters of Rye in 1991 from PMT. Caught in the summer of 1993, it is seen working service 667 to Charing.

An unusual vehicle in the fleet of East Surrey was OHV 208Y, a Wadham Stringer Vanguard-bodied Ford R-series. It was delivered to the Greater London Council in 1982 and served with them and then with Lewisham Council until purchased by East Surrey in 1991. It is seen in East Grinstead in October 1992.

Photographed in Orpington High Street in 1996 heading for Warlingham, J326 PPD is an Optare Metrorider. This vehicle moved to Guernsey in 2000.

Laying over in Redhill bus station in 1995, M151 HPL was one of two Dennis Darts with Plaxton Pointer bodies purchased by East Surrey in 1994, joining two others bought the previous year.

Epsom Coaches expanded into bus operations in the late 1980s. In 1991 they purchased this Optare StarRider, F670 NPG, from East Surrey. It is seen in Cromwell Road, Kingston.

Coming full circle, we arrive back in Guildford, where we see Tillingbourne's F279 HOD. This Plaxton Derwent-bodied Leyland Tiger was new to Brixham Coaches, moving to Thames Transit in Oxford before joining Tillingbourne in 1995. It is seen in Guildford bus station in 1998.

Seen in Guildford bus station on 14 February 1992 is Tillingbourne's H421 GPM, a Dormobile-bodied Mercedes-Benz 709D.

Caught in 1994 at Guildford bus station, K101 XPA was one of two Plaxton Derwent-bodied Volvo B10Ms bought at the end of 1993. It is seen arriving on service 25 from Cranleigh.

The year 1995 saw Tillingbourne operating a tourist service, numbered 448, during the summer. The vehicle used was this 1962 former Western National Bristol SUL, seen here at Guildford station. 280 KTA was most definitely a vehicle of my childhood as I regularly saw these around Taunton during the 1960s.

Ending with the firm we started with, we see Safeguard's N611 WND, a Northern Counties Paladin-bodied Dennis Dart purchased in 1998, leaving Guildford Friary bus station for Park Barn on 23 December of that year.

Thomas of Relubbas in the far west of Cornwall bought D173 LTA from Plymouth Citybus in November 1991. A Reeve Burgess-bodied Dodge S56, it is seen here leaving Penzance bus station on a local town service sometime during 1993.

After standardising on Duple-bodied Leyland Leopards and Tigers for a number of years, Safeguard of Guildford turned to the Leyland Lynx in the 1980s, purchasing four. E298 OMG was the last of the four and is seen here in North Street, Guildford, approaching the bus station on 13 June 1990.

Bibliography

Berry, Howard, *Roselyn of Cornwall, A Celebration of 70 Years' Service: 1947–2017* (Chezbrook Publishing, 2017).

Burnett, George & James, Laurie, *Tillingbourne: The Tillingbourne Bus Story* (Midhurst: Middleton Press, 1990).

James, Laurie, *Safeguard Coaches of Guildford* (Stroud: Amberley Publishing, 2014).

James, Laurie, *Somerset's Buses* (Stroud: Tempus Publishing, 2004).